# VICTORIAN LIFE

*BY*

JOHN GUY

# COUNTRY LIFE

*W*hile new technology and machinery improved the efficiency and profitability of many farms, for most people the industrial revolution of the 18th and 19th centuries was a period of massive upheaval and social change. Many people lost their jobs and their homes, since most houses were tied to their occupations and they were forced to seek work elsewhere.

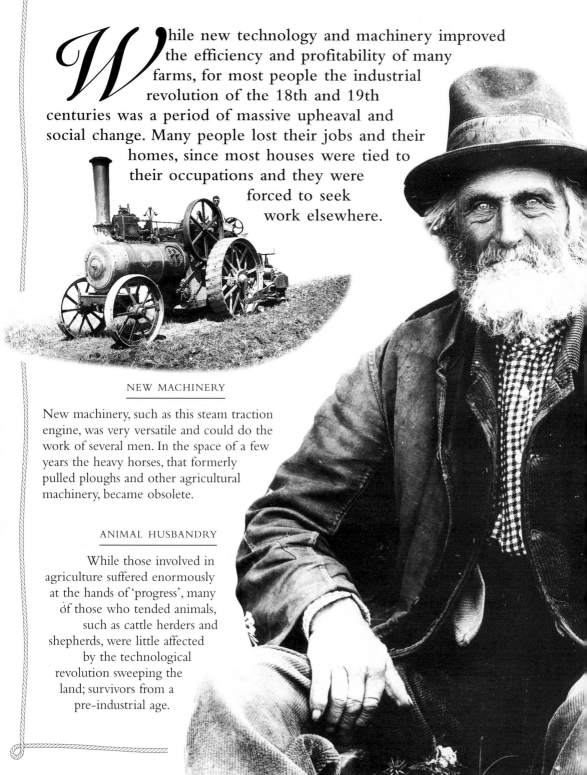

### NEW MACHINERY

New machinery, such as this steam traction engine, was very versatile and could do the work of several men. In the space of a few years the heavy horses, that formerly pulled ploughs and other agricultural machinery, became obsolete.

### ANIMAL HUSBANDRY

While those involved in agriculture suffered enormously at the hands of 'progress', many of those who tended animals, such as cattle herders and shepherds, were little affected by the technological revolution sweeping the land; survivors from a pre-industrial age.

## COUNTRY AIR

Although many of those who worked in the country still lived in primitive, one-roomed cottages, living conditions and sanitation were much better than in town slums.

## CHANGING MARKETPLACE

Many villages lost their weekly market as more and more of the food produced was taken to the towns to feed their burgeoning populations. A single village shop, selling a range of goods, could usually satisfy the needs of most rural communities.

## LIFE EXPECTANCY

Although generally less well-off than town dwellers, those who lived in the country usually had a better quality of life and could expect to live longer; about 50 years of age compared to 40 for those in towns.

## OUR DAILY BREAD

In 1815 Corn Laws had been passed to keep grain prices high and protect England from cheap imports, but these were repealed in 1846 to facilitate free trade. The result was a fall in the price of bread, though farmers were affected badly as a consequence.

# LIFE IN TOWNS

At the beginning of Victoria's reign (1837) only about 20% of the population lived in towns, but by 1901, when she died, this figure had risen to about 75%. During this period the population of Britain doubled from around 20 million to 40 million. Most people moved to towns to find work in the factories. Rows of poor quality terraced slums sprang up around the factories to house them.

## VICTIMS OF CIRCUMSTANCE

Poverty was so bad in most towns that many people resorted to crime in the dingy streets. The old and infirm, particularly, often fell victim to pickpockets.

## POOR SANITATION

Sanitary conditions in Victorian towns were often very poor. Only the rich could afford proper toilet facilities. The poor had to share a communal lavatory, usually just a shed over a hole in the ground treated with quicklime to dissolve effluent. Few houses had running water or drains and it was a daily task to empty slops down open gullies in the streets.

## HOMELESSNESS

Homelessness was a constant problem in towns, especially for those who were unable to work, who were literally put out onto the streets. Alcohol was cheap (beer was less than 1p per pint) and easier to acquire than good drinking water, so drunkenness was a problem, even amongst children.

## STREET TRADERS

The streets offered numerous opportunities to earn a living. Traders sold their wares, such as bread, milk and pies, from hand carts. Girls might sell cut flowers while boys might offer fresh poultry or a shoe shine.

## COMPARATIVE LIFESTYLES

These two views show the comparison between the poor and wealthy sectors of 19th century towns. The rich could afford elegant, well-built villas, while the poor had to tolerate the squalor of cramped, back-to-back housing surrounded by noise and filth.

# LIFE FOR THE RICH

For many wealthy young ladies life was an endless round of social gatherings, attending balls, the opera or the theatre, so as to be seen by prospective husbands.

The Victorian age saw the emergence of a new tier of social class, wealthy businessmen who made vast fortunes from the new advances in technology, though often at the expense of the working classes who were forced to work in appalling conditions for low wages. Until the rise of the Victorian industrial entrepreneurs, most of the country's wealth lay in land ownership, particularly the estates of the aristocracy, but now any enterprising individual could become rich.

A STITCH IN TIME

New technology and mass-production brought many labour-saving devices, including the sewing machine, invented in 1851 by Singer. This sewing machine, manufactured by Wheeler and Wilson, is considered to be the forerunner of the modern lock-stitch and revolutionised clothes manufacture.

QUEEN VICTORIA

- *Born 1819*
- *Ascended the throne 1837*
- *Died 1901*

Victoria was proud of the technical achievements of her reign and allowed many new devices to be used in the royal household, such as electric lighting and carpet cleaners.

## CHARITY STATUS

A charity matinée for a light comedy performance at the Theatre Royal, in London's Haymarket. Theatre-going in general was very fashionable, but it soon became popular, and almost essential for social advancement, to be seen at charitable events.

## FINE TABLEWARE

Fine porcelain and bone china tableware became extremely fashionable among the aristocracy and rising middle-classes. Improved methods of manufacture meant that items could be mass-produced, but retained their 'hand-made' quality.

## THE SPOKEN WORD

The phonograph, the forerunner of today's hi-fi, was invented by Thomas Edison in 1877. Apart from the recording of music one of the earliest uses suggested by Edison was talking books for the blind.

# THE POOR AT HOME

*A*lthough the technological revolution brought wealth to industrialists, it brought abject poverty to the working classes. Many were forced to work long hours, under appalling conditions, for low wages. Many chose to emigrate to Australia, America and Canada. One way out of the poverty trap was to work in service in the houses of the wealthy. There were over one million domestic servants in 1851 out of a population of just 20 million.

## DESTITUTION

Many of the homeless lived in workhouses where, in payment for working during the day, they received a meal and a bed. This old woman was so destitute that she could not work and slept on the steps of the workhouse. She minded a friend's baby in return for food.

## CHILDREN'S HOMES

Homelessness was an ever-growing problem in towns, particularly among children, whose parents might have died. Dr. Thomas Barnado opened his first home for poor boys (many of whom had run away to escape the cruelty of factory conditions) in London in 1870, providing them with food and shelter.

## PAWNBROKERS

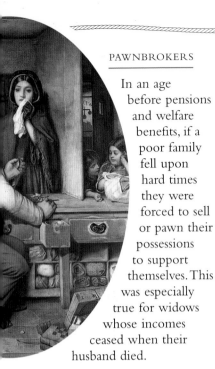

In an age before pensions and welfare benefits, if a poor family fell upon hard times they were forced to sell or pawn their possessions to support themselves. This was especially true for widows whose incomes ceased when their husband died.

## LEARNING BY ROTE

Few working class children received any education because it was felt it would make them discontent with their lot. The fortunate few went to dame schools, charitable institutions run by women in their own homes, where reading, writing and simple arithmetic were taught.

## COTTAGE INDUSTRIES

It was not uncommon for poor couples to have as many as 9 or 10 children. Although this view shows a typical family with the children at play (probably on a Sunday, the only day of rest) the whole family was expected to work. Even those children not sent out to work in factories and mills had to help support the family by doing chores around the house or making items for sale.

# FOOD & DRINK

One of the biggest problems facing Victorian society was how to feed a population that was growing at an alarming rate. In pre-industrial Britain, the majority of people worked on the land and produced their own food. Most people now worked in factories and had to buy all their food with their wages, marking the beginnings of the modern consumer society.

## DELIVERED TO YOUR DOOR

Milk was delivered straight from the farm. Customers took their jugs out into the street to the milkman, who filled them from large churns.

## SPOILT FOR CHOICE

Never before had such a range of foods been available as cheap imports flooded in from abroad. Even the meagre diets of the poor gradually improved and became more varied. Such items as tea, for long an expensive luxury, became affordable by all.

## CONVENIENCE FOODS

One of the solutions to keeping food fresh was this dry-air syphon refrigerator (c.1900). Food was chilled by the insulation of ice blocks in an adjoining compartment, which circulated cold air. Towards the end of the Victorian era tinned foods also became available.

## HOME DELIVERIES

In smaller towns, and in villages, street tradesmen still carried their wares from door-to-door. Fresh bread, fish, dairy products and vegetables were often sold this way, but in larger towns, especially towards the end of the 19th century, improved standards of hygiene meant that more and more people bought their food from shops, where it was better protected.

## THE MIDDLE MAN

Markets are a survival from the pre-industrialised age, when few shops existed and buyers and sellers met to exchange goods. At town wholesale markets, like Covent Garden fruit and vegetable market in London, shown here, larger traders bought goods in bulk from several suppliers at cheaper prices, which they then sold on to smaller traders for a profit.

# PASTIMES

## A GAME FOR GENTLEMEN

Cricket, first played in the 16th century, grew in popularity and became a gentleman's pursuit. W.G. Grace, perhaps the most famous cricketer of all time, lifted the game to its present status. He had an active playing career of 35 years and on one occasion amassed the score of 224 not out.

or most people Sunday was the only day when they did not have to work, so many simply rested. For others, cheap railway transport meant that for the first time they could visit other areas. Day trips to seaside towns became popular, as did visits to the growing number of public art galleries and museums.

## CHILDREN'S ENTERTAINMENT

Children in rural areas were sometimes treated to a performance by a travelling puppeteer with his 'Punch and Judy' show, a survival from medieval fairs.

## THE NOUVEAU RICH

The wealth generated by industry created a new breed of entrepreneurs who amassed large, disposable incomes. Gambling had always been popular, but exclusive casinos and gentlemen's clubs were established in an attempt to legitimise the pursuit.

## I SAY, I SAY, I SAY ....

Every town could boast at least one, in many cases several, theatres and music halls, showing everything from variety shows to plays, opera and ballet. In the 1890s over 350 music halls opened in London alone.

THE DAY OF SETTLEMENT

These characters are settling their debts at the Derby. Gambling on sporting events has always been popular, but never more so than in Victorian times. It was one of the rare occasions when people from different backgrounds mixed socially.

## TRADITIONAL SKILLS

Traditional needlework and embroidery skills remained the main pastime for many middle and upper class ladies. This design has been used for the title page of a children's book on dolls' houses, the manufacture of which became extremely popular in Victorian times.

## BESIDE THE SEASIDE

Although the benefits of sea bathing had been discovered in the 18th century, it was the coming of the railway age that made seaside excursions possible for the masses.

# FASHION

As is the case in all ages, clear distinctions were drawn between the fashions worn by people from different social backgrounds. The poor invariably wore clothes that were practical, giving few concessions to fashion, while the rich could afford better materials and indulge themselves in more elaborate styles, purely for the look, even though many were extremely uncomfortable to wear. People from all classes tended to keep a special set of clothes for Sunday best.

### A FULLER FIGURE

By about 1870 bustles replaced crinoline. Skirts were draped over a frame of padded cushions to give more fullness to the back of the dress.

### FASHION CONSCIOUSNESS

Narrow waists were very fashionable for ladies, right up to the end of Victoria's reign. This was achieved by wearing corsets made of steel, wood or bone, which were so tightly laced that they restricted breathing, causing some women to faint.

## FASHION ACCESSORIES

Ladies carried many fashion accessories, particularly when attending social functions. In addition to jewellery, they might carry a fan, such as the one shown here, complete with artificial flower decoration. Hair styles were more elaborate, often incorporating wigs and false hair pieces. Gentlemen usually carried gloves and a walking cane.

## FOLLOWERS OF FASHION

Working class children wore cast-offs or cut-down adult clothes, while wealthier families dressed their children very formally in miniature versions of adult styles. Boys and girls both wore dresses until about five years old.

## CHANGING FACE OF FASHION

The invention of the sewing machine did not make seamstresses, tailors and shoemakers redundant (in 1891 over a quarter of a million people worked in clothes manufacture) but instead made more elaborate designs possible. Ladies' shoes in particular became far more daring in their design as a result of mechanisation. Gentlemen wore spats, short cloth gaiters below their trouser bottoms to protect their shoes from mud.

## COSTUME JEWELLERY

Many precious and semi-precious stones were imported from the east, particularly from India, where they were quite common, and used to decorate items of fashion jewellery.

# ART &
# ARCHITECTURE

*V*ictorian art and architecture was often dismissed as contributing nothing new and original. While they did produce the Gothic and Classical revivals, the development of graceful structures, such as bridges and canopies using iron, steel and glass are wholly their own. Literary giants like Charles Dickens, Sir Walter Scott and the Brontë sisters developed the novel to its full potential, while probably the most original group of English painters, the Pre-Raphaelites, emerged during this time when Millais, Rossetti, Hunt and other like-minded artists formed a school of art that reflected the spirit of the age.

### SPOKESMAN
### FOR THE AGE

Charles Dickens (1812-70) was the greatest and most popular novelist of his day. His graphic descriptions of Victorian England give us a good idea of what life was really like, particularly for the poor. All of his books were serialised, making them available to all classes.

### THE CRYSTAL PALACE

The Great Exhibition of 1851 was the brainchild of Prince Albert and was housed in the purpose-built Crystal Palace. It was a masterpiece of cast iron and glass, designed by Joseph Paxton, covering 26 acres and measuring three times the length of St. Paul's Cathedral. Incredibly, the building survived a move from Hyde Park to Sydenham after the exhibition, but sadly burned down in 1936.

## EDUCATING THE MASSES

Many art galleries and museums opened in towns throughout Britain to educate the masses and introduce ordinary people to the wider world of art.

## TRAGIC GENIUS

The Brontë sisters, Anne, Emily and Charlotte, all wrote under male pseudonyms to improve their chances of success. They lived in lonely isolation on the Yorkshire moors and died within seven years of one another, all at young ages.

# HEALTH & MEDICINE

The main health problem facing Victorians, particularly in the towns, was that of overcrowding and the public health problems associated with it. The large numbers of people living in the densely packed slum houses produced a lot of waste, but there was no proper means to dispose of it. Streets became open sewers which led to many outbreaks of diseases such as typhoid and cholera. A series of Public Health Acts from 1848 on were passed in Parliament making it the responsibility of local councils to provide drainage and clean water supplies and clear away slums.

## THE WATER CLOSET

As sewerage systems improved so flushable toilets became more common in rich households. The poor usually shared a communal 'earth closet' outside, which was often relocated as the cesspit beneath it filled with effluent.

## MEDIEVAL CURES

Prior to the discovery in around 1856 by such scientists as Louis Pasteur that disease was caused by microscopic bacteria, medical knowledge had advanced little since the middle ages. Crude treatments, like blood-letting to remove toxins, were still widely practiced.

## SHOCK TACTICS

In 1867 Joseph Lister developed an antiseptic to kill bacteria, which increased the survival rate from surgery dramatically. Prior to that over half of patients died from shock, gangrene or secondary infections.

THE EXPRESS DAIRY COMP. L.D
Branches in all parts.

COLLEGE FARM, FINCHLEY.

## POOR DIET

Many children, deprived of sunlight and clean air, and fed a poor, unbalanced diet, developed rickets, a debilitating disease causing bone malformation. Fresh milk containing plenty of vitamin D helped reduce the incidence of the disease.

Following numerous outbreaks of typhoid and cholera in overcrowded towns, a link was discovered by Edwin Chadwick between disease and poor living conditions. Massive sewers were constructed to improve the drainage and carry dirty water out to sea.

DENTAL HYGIENE

This Victorian dentist's surgery shows treadle-operated drills. The successful use of chloroform as an anaesthetic after 1847 made it possible to remove teeth or perform operations painlessly.

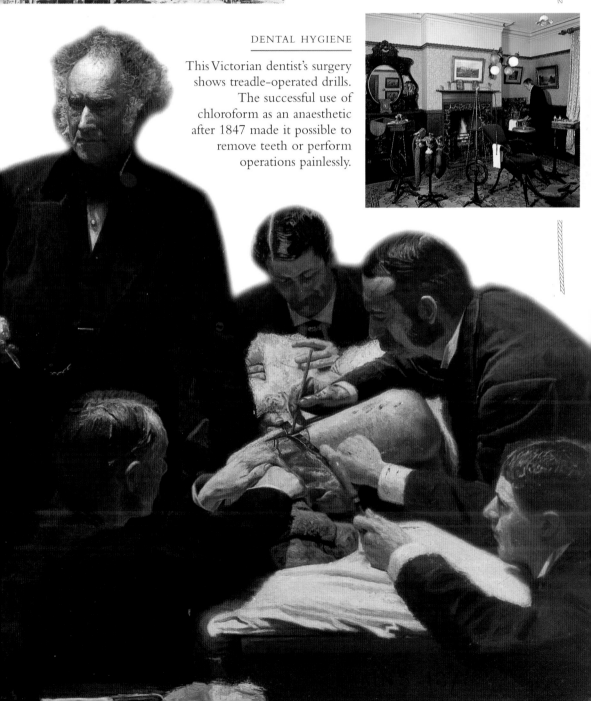

# LOVE & MARRIAGE

**W**omen from all classes were expected to marry young (usually about age 18) and to raise a family and so were not considered eligible for a career. Upper and middle class girls were usually chaperoned when meeting young men. If a woman had a child out of wedlock she was scorned by society and might become a social outcast, forced to enter a workhouse in order to survive.

## ARRANGED MARRIAGES

Few marriages were love matches, but were arranged by parents who chose a suitable spouse for their children.

## OFF TO THE WARS

With so many servicemen deployed around the Empire, many wives were forced to bring up the family single-handed. This picture shows a wife saying farewell to her husband on the eve of his embarkation.

## WILD OATS

Young men from wealthy families were often expected to gain sexual experience from liaisons with women of a lower social order, but marriage between people from different classes was frowned upon and might lead to disinheritance from the family estate.

## A SPINSTER'S LIFE

Unmarried women were regarded as the property of their fathers, who could also claim any wages they earned. Most parents, however, wanted to see their children married off, particularly daughters, who might have no means of support should anything happen to their fathers.

## ROYAL PROPOSAL

According to the dictates of royal protocol, no man is allowed to propose to a queen, so Victoria had to ask for Albert's hand in marriage, unusual for the day. She is seen here surrounded by her children and grandchildren.

# WOMEN & CHILDREN

*L*ife for women and children in the 19th century was unbearably hard and few born to poverty had the opportunity to better themselves. Social reformers, like Lord Shaftesbury, did much to improve things and a series of Acts were passed in the 1840s reducing working hours to 10 a day and improving conditions, but unscrupulous employers continued to exploit their workforce.

## LIFE OF EASE

While boys from wealthy families were groomed for a profession, girls were not expected to work. They spent much of their time entertaining or making social calls to friends and neighbours.

## COMPULSORY EDUCATION

In 1870 the government passed an Education Act stating that all children between the ages of 5–10 must attend school. The education was not free and many poorer families could not afford to send their children. After 1891 schooling became free to all.

## VALUABLE 'COMMODITIES'

Women of all classes were regarded as the property of their husbands, as were any wages they earned. Until the Property Act of 1882 all of a woman's property automatically belonged to her husband.

## IMPRISONED BY CIRCUMSTANCE

Many women were forced to take their children to prison with them if convicted of a crime, rather than abandon them. Prison reformer Elizabeth Fry helped to improve the often squalid conditions inside and set up schools for the children.

## PRISONERS IN THEIR OWN HOMES

The years of innocence in Victorian childhood were short-lived. Children were considered the property of their father, who could send them out to work as young as five years old and keep all their wages to help support the family. Children could be imprisoned in their own homes, a right husbands had even over their wives until 1891.

## WOMEN'S EQUALITY?

Women had few rights in 19th century Britain and had to perform the same tasks as men at work, but for much less pay. These ladies were photographed at an iron foundry in South Wales in 1865.

# WAR & WEAPONRY

S till basking in the reflected glory of Waterloo, the British were unprepared for the harsh realities of the Crimean War with Russia (1854-56). Afterwards Britain concentrated its military efforts on either extending or defending the realms of the Empire, which covered one quarter of the world's land mass, the largest empire ever known.

## HONOURABLE DISCHARGE

Methods of warfare changed drastically during the 19th century as new technology developed more efficient weapons, such as this rapid-firing gatling gun of 1870. Mechanisation had the effect of dehumanising warfare which, until then, had always been considered an honourable pursuit.

## EMPIRE BUILDING

With increased poverty and unemployment at home, there was no shortage of volunteers to sign up for the many military campaigns of Victoria's empire-building reign; better to risk your life and die with honour than to die destitute.

## THE INDIAN MUTINY

Since the 18th century the East India Company had administered India, with help from the army, supplemented by Indian troops. In 1857 the native troops, supported by many Indian princes, rebelled against British rule. The rebellion was crushed and afterwards India was placed under direct rule of the British government.

## GUERRILLA WARFARE

In 1899 war broke out in South Africa between Dutch settlers, the Boers, and the British. A massive army was sent to crush them, but it proved ineffective against the Boers' guerrilla tactics. Scarcely a victory for the British, peace was eventually achieved in 1902.

## DETERRENT

Alfred Nobel, a Swedish scientist, invented dynamite and other explosive substances, for use in civil engineering projects and as a deterrent to promote world peace. However, military authorities, including Britain, used them to make weapons, such as these sea mines used to blow up ships.

## VALLEY OF DEATH

The 'Charge of the Light Brigade' at Balaclava in the Crimea in 1854, was one of Britain's worst military disasters. Confused orders and incompetent officers culminated in a futile charge straight towards the massed Russian guns. Nearly half of the 673 cavalrymen died or were wounded.

# CRIME & PUNISHMENT

**W**ith so much poverty and such appalling living conditions, many people turned to crime as a way of life. Punishments were severe, even for children, who might be imprisoned for stealing a loaf of bread. Prisons were so overcrowded that 'hulks' were moored in river estuaries to house the overspill. Many convicts were sent to the colonies to serve out their sentences.

INDECENT ASSAULT

Victorians were sensitive to moral standards; this music hall dancer was imprisoned for three months on the grounds of indecency for wearing this costume in public.

## ROYAL SCAPEGOAT

Many people blamed Victoria herself for their hardships and several attempts were made on her life. This attempt was by an out-of-work Irishman in 1849.

## DEATH PENALTY

At the beginning of the 19th century over 200 crimes were punishable by death. Despite reforms, there were still over 70 crimes carrying the death sentence in Victorian times, including petty theft and assault.

## WHEEL OF MISFORTUNE

Conditions inside Victorian prisons were cramped and primitive. Treadmills, similar to the one shown here, were used as a form of exercise or to punish unruly prisoners.

## A POLICEMAN'S LOT

Until the reform bills of Sir Robert Peel in the 1820s, when a proper civilian police force was set up in London, many criminals got away unpunished. By early Victorian times most towns had their own police force to apprehend villains, often recruited from the armed services and run along similar lines.

# TRANSPORT & SCIENCE

**B**ritain's scientists and engineers led the world with their array of technological inventions, such as the development of steam and internal combustion engines, electricity and building techniques. Many of the familiar household objects today, such as light bulbs, typewriters, packaged food and hi-fi had their origins in the Victorian age. Britain became known as the 'workshop of the world'.

## SMILE!

Cameras, first developed in the 19th century, were for the first time in history able to record events as they happened, though initially they were used as reconnaissance aids by the military.

## IMPROVED ROADS

The first motor cars (invented c.1865) resembled horseless carriages and were open to the elements. They needed metalled surfaces to run effectively, which led to road improvements with the development of tarmacadamed surfaces.

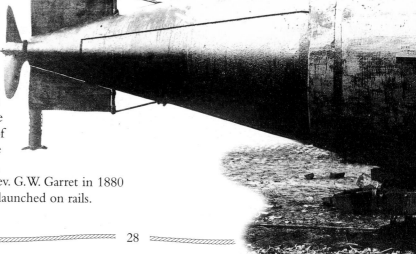

## UNDERWATER TACTICS

The development of the submarine and self-propelled torpedoes in both Britain and France changed the face of modern warfare. The one shown here, invented by the Rev. G.W. Garret in 1880 was launched on rails.

ON THE RIGHT TRACK

The Victorian age saw the rapid development of railways. For the first time in history fast, cheap transport was available to the masses, giving greater mobility to the population. Between 1829 and 1900, 22,000 miles of track were laid in Britain and in 1863 the world's first underground railway was opened in London.

## MASS-PRODUCTION

Advancements in technology made it possible to mass-produce economically all manner of items for everyday use that previously had to be individually hand-made at great expense, such as this practical tape measure.

## IT'S GOOD TO TALK

The telephone was invented by Alexander Graham Bell in 1875. Although greeted with enthusiasm, it was very expensive to install and initially only available to the rich. It was not possible to dial to another user directly. Connection had to be through an operator. Businessmen, who could better afford them, saw the potential of telephones and benefited enormously from improved communication links.

# RELIGION

To most Christians, up to Victorian times, the Bible was taken as literal truth and few people questioned its authenticity. When Charles Darwin and others challenged this view with their revolutionary theories of evolution by natural selection, they shattered the beliefs of ordinary people and clergy alike. Many were unable to reconcile their religious feelings with the new scientific theories and Darwin suffered open derision from the public throughout his life.

## CHALLENGE TO THE CHURCH

The biologist Charles Huxley championed Darwin's theories of evolution when the church attacked his views and tried to discredit him as a heretic.

## SUNDAY SCHOOLS

For many working class children, who worked all week, Sunday or charity schools, organised by the church, were the only form of education they received. Apart from learning to read, the only other subject usually taught was Bible studies.

## RELIGIOUS FERVOUR

A religious fervour and strict moral upbringing swept Victorian society, particularly the upper and middle classes. For the first time since the Reformation many new churches were built, or medieval ones restored. At the beginning of Victoria's reign (1837) about 60% of the population regularly went to church on Sundays; today the figure is less than 1%.

## THE DESCENT OF MAN

When Charles Darwin published 'The Origin of the Species' in 1859 he caused a furore by challenging the biblical account of the Creation, in which God created man in his own likeness. According to Darwin, man evolved gradually from an ape-like creature over many thousands of years.

## THE 'SALLY ARMY'

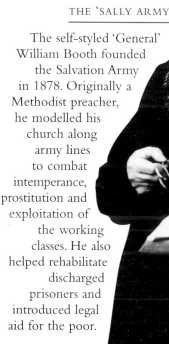

The self-styled 'General' William Booth founded the Salvation Army in 1878. Originally a Methodist preacher, he modelled his church along army lines to combat intemperance, prostitution and exploitation of the working classes. He also helped rehabilitate discharged prisoners and introduced legal aid for the poor.

## THE OXFORD MOVEMENT

Evangelicalism had its origins in Oxford. A group of like-minded men felt that the Anglican Church had become lax in its duties towards the poor and so formed a new church with a more humanitarian doctrine.

# A GLOSSARY OF INTERESTING TERMS

**Char** - A word introduced into the English language from the days when the British Empire extended into much of Asia. Now a slang word for a cup of tea, it comes from the chinese word for tea, *cha*.

**Co-operative** - The chain of modern stores known as co-operatives (or co-ops) had their origins in Lancashire in 1844, when a group of weavers, co-operating with one another, opened a grocery store that shared its profits with their customers in the form of a dividend.

**Dickensian** - A term originally applied to the characters of Charles Dickens novels, but now used to describe anything of a primitive or poor quality, particularly in relation to social conditions.

**Jodhpurs** - these close-fitting trousers, still used when riding horses today, were first introduced in Victorian times from Jodhpur, in India, where they formed part of the traditional dress.

**Pasteurised** - The treatment known as pasteurisation to kill germs in food and drink takes its name from the French scientist Louis Pasteur, who discovered the link between bacteria and disease in 1856.

**Strike** - In 1888 women working in a London match factory withdrew their labour to get better working conditions. The word *strike* (from striking a match) is now used to describe similar industrial actions.

**Victoria Cross** - the highest military decoration for conspicuous bravery was first instituted by Victoria herself in 1856.

## ACKNOWLEDGEMENTS

We would like to thank: Graham Rich, Tracey Pennington, Liz Rowe and Peter Done for their assistance.

Copyright © 1997 ticktock Publishing Ltd.

First published in Great Britain by ticktock Publishing Ltd., Great Britain. All rights reserved.

No part of this publication may be reproduced, stored in a retrieval system, or transmitted in any form or by any means, electronic, mechanical, photocopying, recording or otherwise, without prior written permission of the copyright owner.

Printed in Italy

Acknowledgements: Picture Credits  t=top, b=bottom, c=centre, l=left, r=right, OFC=outside front cover, IFC=inside front cover, IBC= inside back cover, OBC= outside front cover.

The Games Room, 1889, Jean Beraud © ADAGP, Paris and DACS, London 1997 (Musee Carnavalet, Paris/Giraudon/Bridgeman Art Library, London); 12/13b. By courtesy of BT Archives; 29cr & OBC. B.T. Batsford Ltd; 6/7b. Barnado's Photographic Archive (D58); 8bl & OBC. The Beamish. The North of England Open Air Museum; 19cr. Bodleian Library, University of Oxford: John Johnson Collection; Political General folder 1; 4l, 5br & 32, Trades and Professions 6; 4/5b, Educational 16; 9tr, Trade in Prints and Scraps 9; 13cl, Trade in Prints and Scraps 7; 18l & OBC, Food 2; 18cb, Alphabets 3; 30/31t. Sheffield City Art Galleries/Bridgeman Art Library, London; OFCc. FORBES Magazine Collection, New York/Bridgeman Art Library, London; 6bl & OBC, 21cr, 31tr. Christopher Wood Gallery, London/Bridgeman Art Library, London; 9tl; 12/13b. Marylebone Cricket Club, London/Bridgeman Art Library, London; 12l & OFC. Jefferson College, Philadelphia/Bridgeman Art Library, London; 19b. Guildhall Art Gallery, Corporation of London/ Bridgeman Art Library, London; 20b. Mary Evans Picture Library; 3tl, 3tr, 3c, 5tl, 5tr, 12cr, 13cr, 16tl & OBC, 22/23c, 23tr & OFC, 23cr, 24l & OFC, 24/25c & OBC, 25t, 25cr, 26tl, 26/27b & OBC, 27tr & OBC, 28r & OFC. By courtesy of Fine Art Photographic Library; 15tr, 16/17b, 17t, 20tl, 25c, 25b, 29t, 30b. Galerie Berko/Fine Art Photographic Library; 8/9b, 11t. Haynes Fine Art/Fine Art Photographic Library; 6t. Hollywood Road Gallery/Fine Art Photographic Library; 14bl. N.R. Omell Gallery/Fine Art Photographic Library; 7r. Polak Gallery/Fine Art Photographic Library; 13t, 22tl, 22bl. Sutcliffe Galleries/Fine Art Photographic Library; 3br, 21tl. Guildhall Library, Corporation of London; 5c, 10br. From The John Hillelson Collection; 8tl, 26cr. Hulton Getty; 2l, 7tl, 14tl, 19tl, 21br, 27cl, 30tl. Hunting Aerofims Ltd (Mills 147); 13br & OFC. The Illustrated London News Picture Library; 27tl. Museum of London; IFC/1, 14/15t, 14/15b & OFC, 15br. By courtesy of the National Portrait Gallery, London; 17cr. Oxfordshire Photographic Archive, DLA, OCC; 2r, 10l, 31bl. Popperfoto; 23br. Rural History Centre, University of Reading; 11cb. The Salvation Army International Heritage Centre; 31br. Science Museum/Science & Society Picture Library; 6/7c & OBC, 11cl, 18tr, 28tl & OFC, 28/29b, 29c.

Every effort has been made to trace the copyright holders and we apologise in advance for any unintentional omissions. We would be pleased to insert the appropriate acknowledgement in any subsequent edition of this publication.

A CIP Catalogue for this book is available from the British Library. ISBN 1 86007 005 1